GW01424141

contents

NZ, Canada, US and UK readers
Please note that Australian cup and
spoon measurements are metric.
A conversion chart appears on page 62.

Egg Essentials

Eggs are the ultimate fast food: they cook in minutes, are far more nutritious than a burger or fries, can be eaten at any hour of the day, are inexpensive – and you don't have to leave your house or stand in a queue to satisfy your hunger.

An egg contains the highest quality proteins, is high in both vitamins and minerals and, of its average 6 grams of fat, has only 2 grams of saturated fat. And while once believed to contribute to high cholesterol, CSIRO research has shown most people can eat two eggs a day and show little or no increase in cholesterol levels.

Shell colour is determined by the breed of hen and what it has been fed; it has nothing to do with quality. These days there is a variety of eggs to choose from, including cage, barn laid, free range, omega 3, organic and vegetarian eggs – and, while cost and taste are considerations, the decision as to which egg to buy is an individual preference.

Leave eggs in their carton and store it in the refrigerator as soon as you bring them home to slow down deterioration. The carton helps reduce water loss from the eggs and protects them from absorbing flavour from other refrigerated items. Most eggs can be kept, in their carton, for up to four weeks.

The best egg is as fresh an egg as possible. If in doubt, cover an uncooked egg with cold water in a medium bowl: if it sinks, it's fresh; if it floats, don't use it. Never use an egg that is already cracked when you reach for it.

You can get some indication of how fresh an egg is when you break it into the frying pan. Older eggs will have a stronger smell and the white will be thin and spread in the pan. A fresh egg has a distinctly thick yolk and the white will stay as a contained oval. If a recipe calls for more than one egg, break one egg into a small cup, then add it to the mix; repeat with remaining eggs. That way, if an egg is stale, you can discard it.

POACHED EGG Bring water to a boil in small frying pan; break egg into small bowl or cup then slide egg into the pan. As soon as the water returns to a boil; cover pan. Turn off heat; stand about 2 minutes or until a light film of white has set over the yolk. If you cover the pan with a glass lid you can keep an eye on the poaching process. Don't lift the lid during the poaching time as the steam helps cook the egg.

CODDLED EGG Bring water to a boil in small saucepan; using slotted spoon, carefully lower whole egg into the water. Cover pan tightly, remove from heat; using slotted spoon, remove egg from water after 1 minute. When cool enough to handle, crack egg into small bowl or directly onto the toast or salad, etc, that you're eating it with.

BOILED EGG Cover egg with cold water in small saucepan, cover pan; bring water to a boil, uncover pan. Stirring the egg will centralise the yolk. Timing the egg is a personal matter but, for a 60g egg, about 3 minutes will result in a soft-boiled egg with a runny yolk and just-set white; 5 minutes will produce an egg having a firm white and yolk just about solid; while 8 minutes will result in a hard-boiled egg.

To shell hard-boiled eggs, as soon as you remove them from the boiling water, crack the shells all over and immediately plunge eggs into a bowl of cold water for at least 2 minutes. This helps prevent that ugly dark circle forming around the yolk, halts further cooking and speeds up the cooling process, making the eggs easier to shell.

spinach scrambled egg

20g butter
75g spinach leaves
8 slices pancetta
8 eggs
½ cup (125ml) light cream
4 slices crusty bread

1 Heat half of the butter in large non-stick frying pan. Add spinach; cook until spinach just wilts. Drain on absorbent paper; cover to keep warm.
2 Grill pancetta until crisp; cover to keep warm.
3 Whisk eggs and cream in medium bowl until combined.
4 Heat remaining butter in same cleaned pan over medium heat. Add egg mixture; wait a few seconds, then, using a wide spatula, gently scrape the set egg mixture along the base of the pan; cook until creamy and just set.
5 Meanwhile, toast bread. Top toast with pancetta, scrambled eggs and spinach.

serves 4
per serving 25.7g total fat (11.7g saturated fat); 1559kJ (373 cal); 14.4g carbohydrate; 21.7g protein; 1.1g fibre
tips Recipe best made just before serving.
You will need about half a bunch of spinach for this recipe.
on the table in 15 minutes

creamy scrambled egg on brioche with crispy bacon

250g cherry tomatoes
1 tablespoon olive oil
8 slices thin bacon
8 eggs
½ cup (125ml) cream
2 tablespoons finely chopped fresh chives
30g butter
4 slices brioche, toasted

1 Preheat grill.
2 Toss tomatoes in oil. Cook bacon and tomato under grill until bacon is crisp and tomato skins start to split. Cover to keep warm.
3 Meanwhile, combine eggs, cream and chives in medium bowl; beat lightly with fork.
4 Heat butter in large non-stick frying pan over medium heat. Add egg mixture, wait a few seconds, then use a wide spatula to gently scrape the set egg mixture along the base of the pan; cook until creamy and just set.
5 Serve brioche topped with egg, bacon and tomatoes.

serves 4
per serving 52g total fat (23.9g saturated fat); 3223kJ (771 cal); 40g carbohydrate; 37.6g protein; 2.5g fibre
tip Recipe best made just before serving.
on the table in 25 minutes

mini onion and cheese frittatas

2 tablespoons olive oil
3 medium brown onions (450g), sliced thinly
1 medium red capsicum (200g), sliced thinly
8 eggs
½ cup (125ml) thickened cream
200g provolone cheese, cut into 1cm cubes

1 Preheat oven to moderately hot (200°C/180°C fan-forced). Grease12-hole (⅓-cup/80ml) muffin pan.
2 Heat oil in large frying pan, add onion and capsicum; cook, stirring occasionally, about 15 minutes or until onion is soft.
3 Lightly beat eggs and cream in medium bowl. Divide egg mixture among pan holes; top with onion mixture and cheese. Bake, uncovered, about 15 minutes or until just cooked through.

makes 12
per frittata 15.6g total fat (7.2g saturated fat); 807kJ (193 cal); 3g carbohydrate; 10.6g protein; 0.7g fibre
tip The frittatas can be made several hours ahead and served cold or at room temperature.
on the table in 30 minutes

poached eggs with pancetta and asparagus

4 slices pancetta
400g asparagus
¼ cup (60ml) white vinegar
4 eggs
30g butter, melted
¼ cup (20g) shaved parmesan
freshly ground black pepper

1 Preheat grill.
2 Cook pancetta under grill until crisp.
3 Meanwhile, boil, steam or microwave asparagus until just tender; drain.
4 Fill deep frying pan with 10cm water, add vinegar; bring to a boil. Crack one egg into a cup, pour egg carefully into boiling water; repeat with remaining eggs.
5 Lower heat to a gentle simmer; cook eggs, uncovered, about 4 minutes or until cooked as desired. Remove eggs, one at a time, using a slotted spoon; drain on a plate lined with absorbent paper.
6 Divide asparagus spears among serving plates. Top with crumbled pancetta and poached eggs; drizzle with butter then top with cheese and pepper.

serves 4
per serving 14.9g total fat (7.3g saturated fat); 794kJ (190 cal); 1.2g carbohydrate; 12.8g protein; 1g fibre
on the table in 30 minutes

potato rösti with poached eggs and chilli relish

2 medium potatoes (400g), peeled, grated coarsely
½ teaspoon salt
40g butter
¼ cup (60ml) white vinegar
4 eggs
⅓ cup (80ml) sweet chilli relish

1 Combine potato and salt in medium bowl; squeeze out excess liquid.
2 Melt half of the butter in medium non-stick frying pan. Spread potato over pan, flatten. Cook, uncovered, over medium heat until golden underneath; invert onto plate. Melt remaining butter in same pan, carefully slide potato rösti back into pan, uncooked-side down. Cook, uncovered, until browned lightly.
3 Meanwhile, fill deep frying pan with 10cm water, add vinegar; bring to a boil. Crack one egg into a cup, pour egg carefully into boiling water; repeat with remaining eggs. Lower heat to a gentle simmer; cook eggs, uncovered, about 4 minutes or until cooked as desired. Remove eggs, one at a time, using a slotted spoon; drain on a plate lined with absorbent paper.
4 Cut rösti into quarters; serve rösti, topped with eggs, relish and grilled tomato wedges, if desired.

serves 4
per serving 14.3g total fat (7.2g saturated fat); 991kJ (237 cal); 16.4g carbohydrate; 10.3g protein; 1.8g fibre
on the table in 35 minutes

egg-white omelettes

12 egg whites
4 green onions, sliced thinly
¼ cup finely chopped fresh chives
¼ cup finely chopped fresh chervil
½ cup finely chopped fresh flat-leaf parsley
½ cup (60g) coarsely grated cheddar
½ cup (50g) coarsely grated mozzarella

1 Preheat grill.
2 Beat a quarter of the egg white in small bowl with electric mixer until soft peaks form; fold in a quarter of the combined onion and herbs.
3 Pour mixture into heated, lightly oiled 20cm non-stick frying pan; cook, uncovered, over low heat until omelette is just browned lightly on the bottom.
4 Sprinkle a quarter of the combined cheeses on half of the omelette. If necessary, cover pan handle with foil, then place pan under hot grill until cheese begins to melt and omelette sets; fold omelette over to completely cover cheese. Carefully slide onto serving plate; cover to keep warm.
5 Repeat process three more times with remaining egg white, onion and herb mixture, and cheese.
6 Serve with salad leaves, if desired.

serves 4
per serving 7.9g total fat (5g saturated fat); 619kJ (148 cal); 1g carbohydrate; 18.2g protein; 0.7g fibre
on the table in 45 minutes

denver omelettes

10 eggs
⅓ cup (80g) sour cream
2 fresh small red thai
   chillies, chopped finely
2 teaspoons vegetable oil
3 green onions,
   sliced thinly
1 medium green
   capsicum (200g),
      chopped finely
100g leg ham,
   chopped finely
2 small tomatoes (260g),
   seeded, chopped finely
½ cup (60g) coarsely
   grated cheddar

1 Break eggs into large bowl, whisk lightly; whisk in sour cream and chilli.

2 Heat oil in large non-stick frying pan; cook onion and capsicum, stirring, until onion softens. Place onion mixture in medium bowl with ham, tomato and cheese; toss to combine.

3 Pour ½ cup of the egg mixture into same lightly oiled pan; cook, tilting pan, over low heat until omelette is almost set. Sprinkle about ⅓ cup of the filling over half of the omelette; using spatula, fold omelette over to completely cover filling.

4 Pour ¼ cup of the egg mixture into empty half of pan; cook over low heat until almost set. Sprinkle about ⅓ cup of the filling over folded omelette, fold omelette over top of first omelette to cover filling. Repeat twice more, using ¼ cup of the egg mixture each time and ⅓ cup filling, to form one large layered omelette. Carefully slide omelette onto plate; cover to keep warm.

5 Repeat steps 3 and 4 to make second layered omelette, using remaining egg mixture and filling. Cut each denver omelette in half to serve.

serves 4
per serving 31.7g total fat (13.8g saturated fat); 1705kJ (408 cal); 2.8g carbohydrate; 28.7g protein; 0.9g fibre
on the table in 25 minutes

bacon and corn soufflé omelettes

3 bacon rashers, chopped finely
1 clove garlic, crushed
½ medium red capsicum (100g), chopped finely
3 green onions, chopped finely
125g can corn kernels, drained
6 eggs, separated
1 tablespoon water
20g butter
½ cup (60g) grated gruyère or cheddar

1 Cook bacon in medium non-stick frying pan until crisp.
Add garlic, capsicum, onion and corn; cook, stirring,
until softened. Remove from heat; cover to keep warm.
2 Lightly beat egg yolks with the water in large bowl
until combined.
3 Beat egg whites in large bowl with an electric mixer
until soft peaks form. Fold egg whites into egg yolk mixture
in two batches.
4 Preheat grill.
5 Melt half of the butter in pan. Pour half of the egg mixture
into pan, smooth top. Cook over medium heat until browned
underneath. If necessary, cover pan handle with foil, then
place pan under hot grill until top is just set.
6 Spoon half of the corn mixture over omelette, sprinkle
with half of the cheese. Fold omelette over and slide onto
serving plate. Repeat with remaining butter, egg, corn
mixture and cheese.

serves 2
per serving 41.7g total fat (19.2g saturated fat); 2483kJ
(594 cal); 11.8g carbohydrate; 44g protein; 2.5g fibre
on the table in 25 minutes

wok-seared mushroom omelettes

⅓ cup (50g) sliced red capsicum
2 green onions, sliced thinly
1 fresh small red thai chilli, chopped finely
1 cup (80g) bean sprouts
30g shiitake mushrooms, sliced thinly
50g oyster mushrooms, sliced thinly
½ cup firmly packed fresh coriander leaves
12 eggs
2 tablespoons fish sauce
2 teaspoons oyster sauce
⅓ cup (80ml) vegetable oil
2 tablespoons oyster sauce, extra
¼ teaspoon sesame oil
1 tablespoon chopped fresh chives

1 Combine capsicum, onion, chilli, sprouts, mushrooms and coriander in small bowl. Combine eggs and sauces in medium bowl; beat lightly. Add half the vegetable mixture to egg mixture.
2 Heat a quarter of the vegetable oil in wok. When oil is just smoking, add a quarter of the egg mixture then, working quickly using a slotted spoon, push cooked egg mixture in from sides of wok and the uncooked mixture to the outside.
3 When omelette is almost set, sprinkle a quarter of the remaining vegetables over one half of the omelette. Reduce heat to low; cook for 1 minute, folding omelette in half over top of vegetables after 30 seconds. Remove omelette from wok with two lifters; drain on absorbent paper. Keep warm. Repeat three times with remaining egg mixture and vegetables.
4 Serve omelettes drizzled with combined extra oyster sauce and sesame oil; top with chives, and extra coriander and green onion, if desired.

serves 4
per serving 36.9g total fat (7.9g saturated fat); 1910kJ (457 cal); 5.7g carbohydrate; 25.6g protein; 1.9g fibre
on the table in 20 minutes

semi-dried tomato and fetta frittatas

1 tablespoon olive oil
2 tablespoons polenta
8 eggs
½ cup (125ml) thickened cream
½ cup (40g) grated parmesan
2 green onions, chopped
100g semi-dried tomatoes, chopped coarsely
60g baby spinach leaves, chopped coarsely
60g fetta, crumbled

1 Preheat oven to moderate (180°C/160°C fan-forced). Brush a six-hole texas muffin pan (¾-cup/180ml) with half of the oil. Sprinkle polenta inside pan holes to coat the base and sides; shake away excess.
2 Combine egg, cream, parmesan, onions, tomato and spinach in large bowl; mix well.
3 Divide mixture among pan holes, top with fetta; brush fetta with remaining oil.
4 Bake, uncovered, about 25 minutes or until centre is just set.

makes 6
per frittata 36g total fat (16.4g saturated fat); 2011kJ (481 cal); 14.1g carbohydrate; 26g protein; 4.3g fibre
tip The frittatas can be made several hours ahead and served cold or at room temperature.
on the table in 35 minutes

frittata with two toppings

2 tablespoons olive oil
1 medium brown onion (150g), chopped finely
2 tablespoons coarsely chopped fresh flat-leaf parsley
10 eggs
2 tablespoons finely grated parmesan
20g butter
2 cloves garlic, crushed
8 button mushrooms
4 char-grilled artichokes, halved
¼ cup (50g) char-grilled capsicum, sliced thinly

1 Heat oil in medium non-stick frying pan; cook onion, stirring, until soft. Stir in half of the parsley.
2 Combine egg and cheese in large bowl; pour into pan. Cook over low heat, covered loosely, about 8 minutes or until edges are set.
3 Preheat grill.
4 If necessary, cover pan handle with foil then place pan under hot grill until egg mixture is browned lightly and just set. Invert onto a large plate.
5 Meanwhile, heat butter in small non-stick frying pan; cook garlic and mushrooms, stirring, until just tender. Stir in remaining parsley.
6 Cut frittata into 16 wedges, arrange on a serving platter. Top half of the wedges with the mushrooms and half with the combined artichokes and capsicum.

serves 8
per serving 15.7g total fat (4.9g saturated fat); 790kJ (189 cal); 1.4g carbohydrate; 11g protein; 0.5g fibre
tip The frittata can be made several hours ahead and served cold or at room temperature.
on the table in 30 minutes

potato frittata

600g baby new potatoes
1 tablespoon olive oil
1 medium red capsicum (200g)
1 small brown onion (80g)
¼ cup chopped fresh basil
¼ cup chopped fresh flat-leaf parsley
10 eggs
½ cup (40g) grated parmesan

1 Boil, steam or microwave potatoes until just tender; when cool enough to handle, cut potatoes into quarters.
2 Meanwhile, heat oil in large non-stick frying pan; cook capsicum and onion, stirring, until softened.
3 Combine potato, basil, parsley and eggs in large bowl. Pour egg mixture into pan. Cook, over low heat, about 8 minutes or until edges are set.
4 Meanwhile, preheat grill.
5 Sprinkle top with cheese. If necessary, cover pan handle with foil then place pan under hot grill until frittata is just set.

serves 4
per serving 22.9g total fat (7.3g saturated fat); 1647kJ (394 cal); 20.1g carbohydrate; 26.8g protein; 3g fibre
tip The frittata can be made several hours ahead and served cold or at room temperature.
on the table in 30 minutes

eggs ranchero-style

This is our take on the traditional Mexican breakfast dish,
huevos rancheros.

1 small red onion (100g), chopped finely
4 medium tomatoes (600g), chopped coarsely
2 tablespoons water
1 tablespoon balsamic vinegar
1 medium red capsicum (200g), chopped finely
4 eggs
4 corn tortillas, warmed

1 Cook onion in lightly oiled large non-stick frying pan, stirring, until softened. Add tomato, the water and vinegar; bring to a boil. Reduce heat; simmer, uncovered, 15 minutes, stirring occasionally. Add capsicum; cook, uncovered, 5 minutes.
2 Using large shallow mixing spoon, press four shallow depressions into tomato mixture. Working quickly, break one egg into a cup; slide egg into one of the hollows in tomato mixture; repeat with remaining eggs. Cover pan; cook, over low heat, about 5 minutes or until eggs are just set.
3 Divide tortillas among plates. Use egg slide to carefully lift egg and tomato mixture onto each tortilla.

serves 4
per serving 6.7g total fat (1.9g saturated fat); 677kJ (162 cal); 13.9g carbohydrate; 11.2g protein; 3.6g fibre
on the table in 40 minutes

baked eggs with prosciutto and brie

1 tablespoon olive oil
100g prosciutto, chopped finely
100g button mushrooms, chopped finely
4 green onions, chopped finely
100g slightly under ripe brie cheese, chopped coarsely
8 eggs

1 Preheat oven to moderately hot (200°C/180°C fan-forced). Grease four ¾-cup (180ml) shallow ovenproof dishes.
2 Heat oil in medium frying pan; cook prosciutto and mushrooms, stirring, until mushrooms soften.
3 Add onion; cook, stirring, until onion softens. Remove pan from heat; stir in half of the cheese.
4 Divide prosciutto mixture among dishes; break two eggs into each dish.
5 Bake, uncovered, 5 minutes. Increase oven temperature to hot (220°C/200°C fan-forced). Sprinkle remaining cheese over eggs; bake, uncovered, about 5 minutes or until eggs set and cheese melts.
6 Serve immediately with freshly ground black pepper, if desired.

serves 4
per serving 25.3g total fat (9.5g saturated fat); 1388kJ (332 cal); 1.3g carbohydrate; 25.6g protein; 0.9g fibre
on the table in 25 minutes

spaghetti alla carbonara

500g spaghetti
2 tablespoons extra virgin olive oil
250g sliced ham, chopped finely
3 cloves garlic, crushed
3 eggs
½ cup (40g) grated parmesan

1 Cook spaghetti in large saucepan of boiling water, uncovered, until just tender; drain.
2 Meanwhile, heat oil in large frying pan. Add ham; cook, stirring, until browned and crisp. Add garlic; stir until fragrant.
3 Place eggs and cheese in medium bowl; beat with fork until well combined.
4 Return hot pasta to pan, add egg and ham mixtures; toss well.
5 Serve spaghetti immediately, sprinkled with black pepper.

serves 4
per serving 20g total fat (5.7g saturated fat); 2822kJ (675 cal); 85.6g carbohydrate; 34.8g protein; 4.5g fibre
tip This recipe must be made just before serving.
on the table in 20 minutes

zucchini gratin

7 medium zucchini (840g)
60g butter
2 medium brown onions (300g), chopped finely
¼ cup finely shredded fresh basil leaves
3 eggs
¾ cup (180g) crème fraîche or sour cream
¾ cup (90g) grated gruyère cheese

1 Peel five of the zucchini, then coarsely grate all zucchini. Melt half of the butter in large frying pan, add zucchini; cook, stirring, over medium heat, about 10 minutes or until softened and excess liquid is evaporated.
2 Meanwhile, melt remaining butter in medium frying pan; cook onion, over medium heat, stirring, about 5 minutes or until very soft. Add onion and basil to the zucchini; mix well.
3 Preheat oven to moderately hot (200°C/180°C fan-forced). Grease 2-litre (8-cup) shallow ovenproof dish.
4 Whisk eggs, crème fraîche and half of the cheese in medium bowl.
5 Spread zucchini mixture into dish. Top with egg mixture, swirl with a knife to mix lightly. Sprinkle with remaining cheese.
6 Bake, uncovered, about 25 minutes or until browned lightly and just set.

serves 6
per serving 28.1g total fat (17g saturated fat); 1329kJ (318 cal); 6g carbohydrate; 11.2g protein; 3g fibre
on the table in 35 minutes

goat cheese soufflé with creamed spinach sauce

Goat cheese, with its strong, earthy taste, is available in both soft and firm textures, in various shapes and sizes, and is often rolled in ash or herbs.

cooking-oil spray
¼ cup (25g) packaged
    breadcrumbs
30g butter
2 tablespoons plain flour
1 cup (250ml) milk
4 eggs, separated
¼ teaspoon cayenne
    pepper
150g firm goat cheese,
    crumbled
creamed spinach sauce
180g baby spinach leaves
⅔ cup (160ml) cream,
    warmed

1 Preheat oven to moderately hot (200°C/180°C fan-forced). Spray six 1-cup (250ml) soufflé dishes with cooking-oil spray, sprinkle with breadcrumbs; place on oven tray.
2 Melt butter in small saucepan, add flour; cook, stirring, until mixture bubbles and thickens. Gradually add milk; stir until mixture boils and thickens. Transfer to large bowl; quickly stir in egg yolks, pepper and cheese; cool 5 minutes.
3 Beat egg whites in small bowl with electric mixer until soft peaks form; gently fold whites into cheese mixture, in two batches.
4 Divide mixture among dishes; bake, uncovered, about 15 minutes or until soufflés are puffed and browned lightly.
5 Meanwhile, make creamed spinach sauce.
6 Serve soufflés immediately with creamed spinach sauce.

creamed spinach sauce Boil, steam or microwave spinach until just wilted; drain. When cool enough to handle, squeeze out excess liquid. Blend or process spinach until almost smooth. With motor operating, gradually add cream; process until smooth.

serves 6
per serving 25.9g total fat (15.4g saturated fat); 1296kJ (310 cal); 8.7g carbohydrate; 11.6g protein; 0.7g fibre
on the table in 35 minutes

egg salad

1 small french bread stick
2 cloves garlic, crushed
¼ cup (60ml) olive oil
6 bacon rashers (420g), rind removed, sliced thickly
150g mesclun
6 medium egg tomatoes (450g), sliced thinly
4 hard-boiled eggs, halved lengthways
red wine vinaigrette
¼ cup (60ml) red wine vinegar
3 teaspoons dijon mustard
⅓ cup (80ml) extra virgin olive oil

1 Preheat grill.
2 Cut bread into 1cm slices. Brush both sides with combined garlic and oil; toast under grill.
3 Cook bacon in large frying pan until crisp; drain on absorbent paper.
4 Meanwhile, place ingredients for red wine vinaigrette in screw-top jar; shake well.
5 Combine bread and bacon in large bowl with mesclun and tomato, top with egg; drizzle with vinaigrette.

serves 4
per serving 4.4g total fat (8.3g saturated fat); 2370kJ (567 cal); 19.5g carbohydrate; 23.4g protein; 3.5g fibre
on the table in 35 minutes

eggplant egg foo yung

Chinese omelettes are simple to prepare and make a delicious breakfast or light lunch. In this version, we've used bean sprouts, green onion and baby eggplant, but you can substitute any combination of vegetables you like.

1 cup (250ml) chicken stock
1 tablespoon oyster sauce
1 tablespoon dry sherry
1 tablespoon cornflour
¼ cup (60ml) water
10 eggs
4 cups (320g) bean sprouts, chopped coarsely
1 fresh small red thai chilli, chopped finely
2 baby eggplants (120g), chopped finely
4 green onions, sliced thinly
1 tablespoon peanut oil

1 Combine stock, sauce and sherry in small saucepan; bring to a boil. Stir in blended cornflour and water; return to a boil. Boil, stirring, until sauce thickens.
2 Combine eggs, sprouts, chilli, eggplant and three-quarters of the onion in large bowl.
3 Heat oil in large non-stick frying pan; add ½ cup of the egg mixture. Flatten egg mixture with spatula; cook, uncovered, until browned and set underneath. Turn, cook other side. Repeat with remaining egg mixture; you will get eight omelettes.
4 Divide omelettes among serving dishes; drizzle with sauce, top with remaining onion.

serves 4
per serving 18.2g total fat (5g saturated fat); 1154kJ (276 cal); 6.8g carbohydrate; 20.5g protein; 3.3g fibre
on the table in 40 minutes

raspberry soufflés

300g frozen raspberries, thawed
1 tablespoon water
½ cup (110g) caster sugar
4 egg whites
300ml thickened cream
2 teaspoons caster sugar, extra

1 Preheat oven to moderate (180°C/160°C fan-forced). Grease four 1-cup (250ml) ovenproof dishes; place on oven tray.
2 Combine 250g of the raspberries and the water in small saucepan; bring to a boil. Reduce heat; simmer, uncovered, until raspberries soften. Add sugar, stir over medium heat, without boiling, until sugar dissolves; bring to a boil. Reduce heat; simmer, uncovered, about 5 minutes or until mixture is thick and pulpy. Remove from heat; push mixture through fine sieve over small bowl, discard seeds.
3 Beat egg whites in small bowl with electric mixer until soft peaks form. With motor operating, gradually add hot raspberry mixture; beat until well combined. Divide mixture among dishes.
4 Bake, uncovered, about 15 minutes or until soufflés are puffed and browned lightly.
5 Meanwhile, beat remaining raspberries, cream and extra sugar in small bowl with electric mixer until thickened slightly. Serve hot soufflés immediately with raspberry cream.

serves 4
per serving 27.9g total fat (18.2g saturated fat); 1735kJ (415 cal); 36.6g carbohydrate; 6.1g protein; 4.1g fibre
tips Thaw raspberries on absorbent paper in the refrigerator. Soufflés must be served immediately.
on the table in 40 minutes

chocolate soufflés

2 tablespoons caster sugar
200g dark eating chocolate, chopped coarsely
50g butter, chopped
3 egg yolks
7 egg whites
¼ cup (55g) caster sugar, extra
1 tablespoon cocoa powder

1 Preheat oven to moderately hot (200°C/180°C fan-forced).
Grease eight ½-cup (125ml) ovenproof dishes with softened
butter. Place sugar in one of the dishes, turn dish to coat
base and side. Tip excess sugar into next dish; repeat with
all dishes. Place dishes on oven tray.
2 Combine chocolate and butter in large heatproof bowl over
pan of simmering water, ensuring that water does not touch
bottom of bowl; stir until melted. Remove bowl from heat; stir
in egg yolks.
3 Beat egg whites in large bowl with electric mixer until soft
peaks form; gradually add extra sugar, beating until dissolved.
4 Using a large balloon whisk, gently fold one-third of the
egg-white mixture into chocolate mixture, then gently fold
in the remainder of the egg-white mixture.
5 Divide soufflé mixture among dishes; smooth soufflé
tops level with tops of the dishes. Bake, uncovered, about
12 minutes or until soufflés are puffed.
6 Dust soufflés quickly with sifted cocoa; serve immediately,
with vanilla ice-cream, if desired.

serves 8
per serving 15.2g total fat (11g saturated fat); 1066kJ
(255 cal); 25.7g carbohydrate; 5.5g protein; 1.2g fibre
tip This recipe must be made just before serving.
on the table in 30 minutes

grilled sabayon peaches

*Sabayon is a light, foamy custard that has been whisked over
simmering water in order to cook the egg yolks as it thickens.*

6 medium peaches (900g), sliced thickly
4 egg yolks
2 tablespoons caster sugar
2 tablespoons peach liqueur
2 tablespoons apple juice

1 Arrange peach slices in six shallow 1-cup (125ml)
ovenproof serving dishes.
2 Combine egg yolks, sugar, liqueur and juice in large
bowl. Place bowl over pan of simmering water, ensuring
that water doesn't touch bottom of bowl. Whisk constantly
about 8 minutes or until mixture is very thick and creamy.
3 Meanwhile, preheat grill.
4 Spoon warm sabayon evenly over peach slices.
5 Place dishes under grill about 1 minute or until just
browned lightly. Serve immediately.

serves 6
per serving 3.9g total fat (1.2g saturated fat); 564kJ
(135 cal); 17.7g carbohydrate; 3.2g protein; 1.8g fibre
on the table in 25 minutes

warm lemon meringue pots

2 tablespoons cornflour
½ cup (110g) caster sugar
¼ cup (60ml) lemon juice
½ cup (125ml) water
1 teaspoon finely grated lemon rind
2 eggs, separated
30g butter, chopped
2 tablespoons thickened cream
⅓ cup (75g) caster sugar, extra

1 Preheat oven to moderately hot (200°C/180°C fan-forced).
2 Stir cornflour, sugar, juice and the water in small saucepan until mixture boils and thickens. Reduce heat; simmer, uncovered, 1 minute. Remove from heat; stir in rind, egg yolks, butter and cream.
3 Divide lemon mixture among four ½-cup (125ml) ovenproof dishes; place dishes on oven tray.
4 Meanwhile, beat egg whites in small bowl with electric mixer until soft peaks form; gradually add extra sugar, 1 tablespoon at a time, beating until sugar dissolves between additions. Spoon meringue evenly over lemon mixture.
5 Bake, uncovered, about 5 minutes or until meringue is browned lightly.

serves 4
per serving 12.9g total fat (7.4g saturated fat); 1384kJ (331 cal); 51.6g carbohydrate; 4.2g protein; 0.1g fibre
on the table in 25 minutes

sour cherry baked custards

*Sour or morello cherries are available in jars. You can use any
canned fruit of your choice.*

1 cup (200g) drained morello cherries
3 eggs
1 teaspoon vanilla extract
½ cup (110g) caster sugar
2 cups (500ml) hot milk
2 teaspoons custard powder
1 tablespoon cold milk
½ teaspoon ground cinnamon

1 Preheat oven to moderately slow (170°C/150°C fan-forced).
2 Pat cherries dry with absorbent paper; divide among four
shallow ¾-cup (180ml) ovenproof dishes.
3 Whisk eggs, extract and sugar in large jug. Gradually whisk
hot milk into egg mixture.
4 Blend custard powder with cold milk in small bowl until
smooth; whisk into egg mixture. Pour mixture over cherries.
5 Bake, uncovered, about 25 minutes or until just set. Serve
warm or cooled sprinkled with cinnamon.

serves 4
per serving 9.6g total fat (4.7g saturated fat); 1233kJ
(295 cal); 43.6g carbohydrate; 10.5g protein; 0.9g fibre
on the table in 35 minutes

coconut custards with papaya

½ cup (135g) grated
   palm sugar
⅓ cup (80ml) water
3 eggs
⅔ cup (160ml) coconut
   cream
2 tablespoons milk
1 teaspoon vanilla extract
1 large red papaya (580g)
2 teaspoons grated
   lime rind
1 tablespoon lime juice
1 tablespoon grated
   palm sugar, extra

1 Place sugar and the water in small saucepan; cook over low heat until sugar is dissolved.
2 Using a balloon whisk, lightly beat eggs, coconut cream and milk until combined, but not frothy. Gradually whisk hot sugar syrup into egg mixture, then stir in extract. Strain custard into heatproof jug.
3 Pour custard into four ⅔-cup (160ml) heatproof dishes. Place dishes in bamboo steamer, cover dishes with a sheet of baking paper; place lid on steamer; gently steam about 15 minutes or until just set.
4 Meanwhile, peel and seed papaya; cut into quarters. Combine papaya in medium bowl with rind, juice and extra sugar.
5 Cool custards 5 minutes; serve with papaya mixture.

serves 4
per serving 13.5g total fat (9.1g saturated fat); 1492kJ (357 cal); 54.4g carbohydrate; 7.3g protein; 3g fibre
tips The custards can be made several hours ahead and served cold, if desired. Store custards, covered, in refrigerator.
on the table in 35 minutes

floating islands in cardamom cream

2 egg whites
⅓ cup (75g) caster sugar
⅔ cup (160ml) cream
2 teaspoons honey
½ teaspoon ground cardamom
⅓ cup (60g) coarsely chopped pistachios

1 Preheat oven to moderately slow (170°C/150°C fan-forced). Grease four ¾-cup (180ml) ovenproof dishes.
2 Beat egg whites in small bowl with electric mixer until soft peaks form; gradually add sugar, 1 tablespoon at a time, beating until sugar dissolves between additions.
3 Divide egg white mixture among dishes; using spatula, smooth tops. Place dishes in large deep baking dish; pour enough boiling water into baking dish to come halfway up sides of dishes.
4 Bake, uncovered, about 12 minutes or until floating islands have risen by about a third. Stand in baking dish 2 minutes.
5 Meanwhile, combine cream, honey and cardamom in small jug.
6 Divide cardamom cream among serving plates; turn floating islands onto cream, sprinkle with nuts.

serves 4
per serving 25.1g total fat (12.4g saturated fat); 1424kJ (340 cal); 25.2g carbohydrate; 5.5g protein; 1.4g fibre
tip Cardamom cream will intensify in flavour if made a few hours before serving.
on the table in 30 minutes

zabaglione

2 eggs
4 egg yolks
½ cup (110g) caster sugar
⅓ cup (80ml) marsala
12 sponge finger biscuits

1 Place eggs, egg yolks and sugar in large heatproof bowl over pan of simmering water, ensuring that water does not touch bottom of bowl.
2 Using an electric mixer or whisk, beat egg mixture constantly until light and fluffy. Gradually add marsala while continuing to whisk for about 10 minutes or until mixture is thick and creamy.
3 Spoon zabaglione into small serving glasses; serve with sponge finger biscuits.

serves 6
per serving 6.8g total fat (2.1g saturated fat); 970kJ (232 cal); 34g carbohydrate; 6.5g protein; 0.3g fibre
tip Zabaglione must be made just before serving.
on the table in 20 minutes

warm pavlovas with berry compote

3 egg whites
2 cups (320g) icing sugar
½ cup (125ml) boiling water
300ml thickened cream,
    whipped

berry compote

½ cup (125ml) raspberry
    cranberry fruit drink
1 tablespoon lemon juice
¼ cup (55g) caster sugar
1 tablespoon cornflour
1 tablespoon water
500g frozen mixed berries

1 Preheat oven to moderate (180°C/160°C fan-forced). Line large oven tray with baking paper.
2 Beat egg whites, icing sugar and the water in small bowl with electric mixer about 8 minutes or until firm peaks form.
3 Using a large metal spoon, drop six equal portions of mixture onto tray. Bake on the lowest shelf about 25 minutes or until pavlovas are browned lightly and firm to touch.
4 Serve pavlovas immediately, topped with warm berry compote and whipped cream.
berry compote Combine fruit drink, juice and sugar in medium saucepan; stir over heat, without boiling, until sugar is completely dissolved. Add blended cornflour and the water; stir over heat until mixture boils and thickens. Stir in mixed berries.

serves 6
per serving 18.6g total fat (12.1g saturated fat); 1956kJ (468 cal); 73.8g carbohydrate; 3.6g protein; 3.3g fibre
tips The berry compote can be made a day ahead and served cold, or reheated to serve warm with pavlovas. Keep, covered, in refrigerator. Pavlovas must be made close to serving as they will deflate.
on the table in 40 minutes

glossary

bacon rashers also known as slices of bacon, made from pork side, cured and smoked.

basil we used sweet basil unless otherwise specified.

bean sprouts also known as bean shoots; tender new growths of assorted beans and seeds germinated for consumption as sprouts. The most readily available are mung bean, soy bean, alfalfa and snow pea sprouts.

breadcrumbs, packaged fine-textured, crunchy, purchased, white breadcrumbs.

brioche rich, French, yeast bread made with butter and eggs. Available from pâtisseries or specialty bread shops.

butter use salted or unsalted (sweet) butter; 125g is equal to one stick of butter.

capsicum also known as bell pepper or, simply, pepper. Remove seeds and membranes before use.

cardamom can be purchased in pod, seed or ground form. Has a distinctive aromatic, sweetly rich flavour.

cayenne pepper a thin-fleshed, long, extremely hot dried red chilli, usually purchased ground.

cheese

brie often referred to as the "queen of cheeses". Smooth and luxurious, brie has a bloomy white rind and a creamy centre that becomes runnier as it ripens.

cheddar the most common cow-milk "tasty" cheese; should be aged, hard and have a pronounced bite.

fetta Greek in origin; a crumbly textured goat- or sheep-milk cheese with a sharp, salty taste.

goat made from goat milk, has an earthy, strong taste; available in both soft and firm textures, in various shapes and sizes, sometimes rolled in ash or herbs.

gruyère a Swiss cheese having small holes and a nutty, slightly salty, flavour.

mozzarella soft, spun-curd cheese; originated in southern Italy where it is traditionally made from water buffalo milk. Cow-milk versions of this product are now available. It has a low melting point and wonderfully elastic texture when heated and is used to add texture rather than flavour.

parmesan also known as parmigiano, parmesan is a hard, grainy cow-milk cheese which originated in the Parma region of Italy. The curd is salted in brine for a month before being aged for up to two years in humid conditions.

provolone a mild cheese when young, similar to mozzarella. Golden yellow in colour, with a smooth shiny skin.

chervil also known as cicily; mildly fennel-flavoured herb with curly leaves.

chilli available in many different types and sizes. Use rubber gloves when seeding and chopping fresh chillies as they can burn your skin. Removing seeds and membranes lessens the heat level.

sweet chilli sauce the comparatively mild, thai sauce made from red chillies, sugar, garlic and vinegar; used as a condiment more often than in cooking.

thai small, hot and bright red in colour.

cocoa powder also known as cocoa; dried, unsweetened, roasted, ground cocoa beans.

coconut

cream obtained commercially from the first pressing of the coconut flesh alone, without the addition of water; the second pressing (less rich) is sold as the milk. Available in cans and cartons at Asian food stores and supermarkets.

flaked dried, flaked coconut.

coriander also known as pak chee, cilantro or chinese parsley; bright-green leafy herb with a pungent flavour. Both the stems and roots of coriander are also used in Thai cooking; wash well before chopping.

cornflour also known as cornstarch; used as a thickening agent in cooking.

crème fraîche mature fermented cream having a slightly tangy, nutty flavour and velvety texture.

custard powder instant mixture used to make pouring custard; similar to North American instant pudding mixes.

eggs some recipes in this book call for raw or barely cooked eggs; exercise caution if there is a salmonella problem in your area.

fish sauce also known as nam pla or nuoc nam; made from pulverised, salted, fermented fish (most often anchovies) and has a pungent smell and strong taste. There are many versions of varying intensity, so use according to your taste.

flour, plain an all-purpose flour made from wheat.

mesclun a salad mix of assorted young lettuce and other green leaves, including baby spinach leaves, mizuna and curly endive.

morello cherries also known as sour cherries; available from supermarkets in jars.

mushrooms

  button small, cultivated white mushrooms with a mild flavour.

  oyster also known as abalone; grey-white mushroom shaped like a fan. Prized for their smooth texture and subtle, oyster-like flavour.

  shiitake when fresh are also known as chinese black, forest or golden oak mushrooms; have the earthiness and taste of wild mushrooms. Are large and meaty; often used as a substitute for meat in some Asian vegetarian dishes. When dried, they are known as donko or dried chinese mushrooms; rehydrate before use.

oil

  cooking spray we use a cholesterol-free cooking spray made from canola oil.

  olive made from ripened olives. *Extra virgin* and *virgin* are the best.

sesame made from roasted, crushed, white sesame seeds; a flavouring rather than a cooking medium.

vegetable any of a number of oils sourced from plants rather than animal fats.

onion

  green also known as scallion or, incorrectly, shallot; an immature onion picked before the bulb has formed, having a long, bright-green edible stalk.

  red also known as spanish, red spanish or bermuda onion; a sweet-flavoured, large, purple-red onion.

oyster sauce Asian in origin, this rich, brown sauce is made from oysters and their brine, cooked with salt and soy sauce, and thickened with starches.

pancetta cured pork belly; bacon can be substituted.

papaya also known as pawpaw; a large, pear-shaped, red-orange tropical fruit. Sometimes used unripe (green) in cooking.

parsley, flat-leaf also known as continental parsley or italian parsley.

polenta also known as cornmeal; a flour-like cereal made of dried corn (maize), sold ground in several different textures. Also the name of the dish made from it.

prosciutto salt-cured, air-dried (unsmoked) pressed ham; usually sold in paper-thin slices, ready to eat.

spinach also known as english spinach and, incorrectly, silver beet.

sponge finger biscuits also known as savoiardi, savoy biscuits or lady's fingers; Italian-style crisp fingers made from sponge cake mixture.

sugar

  caster also known as superfine or finely granulated table sugar.

  icing sugar also known as confectioners' sugar or powdered sugar.

  palm also known as nam tan pip, jaggery, jawa or gula melaka; made from the sap of the sugar palm tree. Light brown to black in colour and usually sold in rock-hard cakes; substitute it with brown sugar if unavailable.

tortillas thin, round unleavened bread originating in Mexico; purchase vacuum-packed, frozen or fresh. Two kinds are available, one made from wheat flour and the other from corn.

vanilla extract vanilla beans that have been submerged in alcohol. Vanilla essence is not a suitable substitute.

vinegar

  balsamic originally from Modena, Italy, there are now many balsamic vinegars on the market ranging in pungency and quality depending on how, and how long, they have been aged. Quality can be determined up to a point by price; use the most expensive sparingly.

  white made from spirit of cane sugar.

zucchini also known as courgette.

conversion chart

MEASURES

One Australian metric measuring cup holds approximately 250ml, one Australian metric tablespoon holds 20ml, one Australian metric teaspoon holds 5ml.

The difference between one country's measuring cups and another's is within a 2- or 3-teaspoon variance, and will not affect your cooking results. North America, New Zealand and the United Kingdom use a 15ml tablespoon. All cup and spoon measurements are level. The most accurate way of measuring dry ingredients is to weigh them. When measuring liquids, use a clear glass or plastic jug with metric markings.

We use large eggs with an average weight of 60g.

DRY MEASURES

METRIC	IMPERIAL
15g	½oz
30g	1oz
60g	2oz
90g	3oz
125g	4oz (¼lb)
155g	5oz
185g	6oz
220g	7oz
250g	8oz (½lb)
280g	9oz
315g	10oz
345g	11oz
375g	12oz (¾lb)
410g	13oz
440g	14oz
470g	15oz
500g	16oz (1lb)
750g	24oz (1½lb)
1kg	32oz (2lb)

LIQUID MEASURES

METRIC	IMPERIAL
30ml	1 fluid oz
60ml	2 fluid oz
100ml	3 fluid oz
125ml	4 fluid oz
150ml	5 fluid oz (¼ pint/1 gill)
190ml	6 fluid oz
250ml	8 fluid oz
300ml	10 fluid oz (½ pint)
500ml	16 fluid oz
600ml	20 fluid oz (1 pint)
1000ml (1 litre)	1¾ pints

LENGTH MEASURES

METRIC	IMPERIAL
3mm	⅛in
6mm	¼in
1cm	½in
2cm	¾in
2.5cm	1in
5cm	2in
6cm	2½in
8cm	3in
10cm	4in
13cm	5in
15cm	6in
18cm	7in
20cm	8in
23cm	9in
25cm	10in
28cm	11in
30cm	12in (1ft)

OVEN TEMPERATURES

These oven temperatures are only a guide for conventional ovens. For fan-forced ovens, check the manufacturer's manual.

	°C (CELSIUS)	°F (FAHRENHEIT)	GAS MARK
Very slow	120	250	½
Slow	150	275 – 300	1 – 2
Moderately slow	160	325	3
Moderate	180	350 – 375	4 – 5
Moderately hot	200	400	6
Hot	220	425 – 450	7 – 8
Very hot	240	475	9

index

If you like this cookbook, you'll love these...

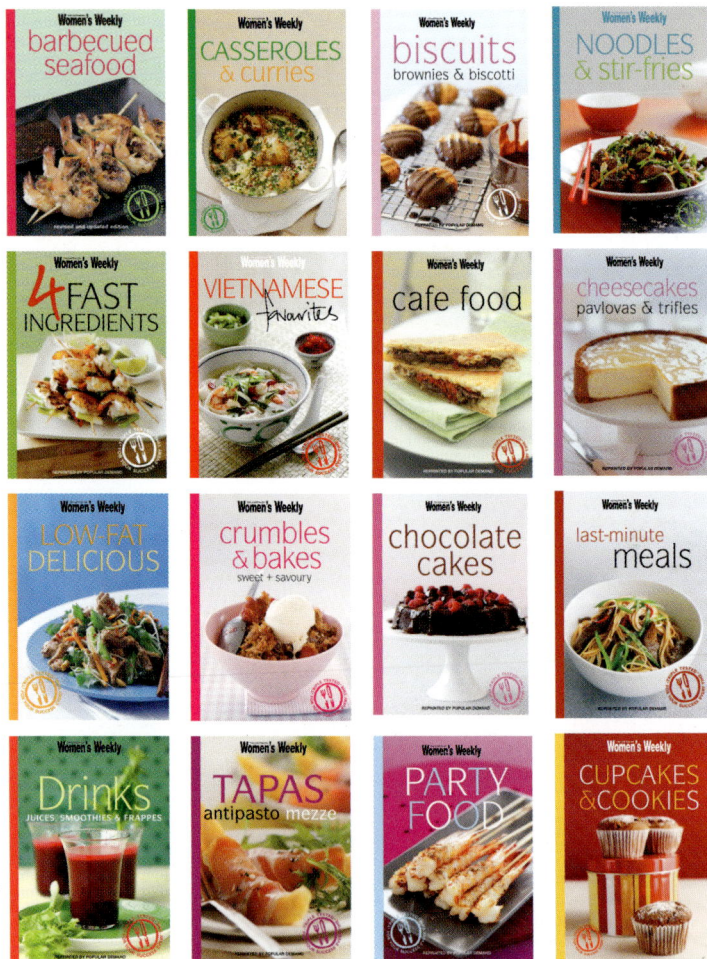

These are just a small selection of titles available in *The Australian Women's Weekly* range
on sale at selected newsagents and supermarkets or online at www.acpbooks.com.au